KINGFISHER
An imprint of Larousse plc
Elsley House, 24–30 Great Titchfield Street,
London W1P 7AD

First published by Kingfisher 1994
2 4 6 8 10 9 7 5 3 1

ISBN 1 85697 244 5

Series editor: Sue Nicholson
Editor: Brigid Avison
Assistant editor: Sara Grisewood
Cover design: Terry Woodley
Design: Ben White Associates
Cover illustrations: Peter Barrett
Peter Barrett's illustrations previously published
in *All About Wild Animals*, Kingfisher 1991
Illustrations on pp 17 & 27 by Maggie Brand
(Maggie Mundy Agency), and on pp 10-11 by Ian Jackson
Typeset by SPAN, Lingfield, Surrey
Printed in Great Britain by BPC Paulton Books Limited

§ 320,968 / 591

£1.99.

Wild Animals

Michael Chinery
Illustrated by Peter Barrett

Kingfisher

Contents

All shapes and sizes

Think of all the different kinds of animals you know – they are all sorts of shapes and sizes. Some are big like elephants, others are fierce like tigers. Wild animals are not all big and scary though – a butterfly is a wild animal, too.

A butterfly is small and delicate . . .

. . . a tiger is large and fierce.

What's a wild animal?

A wild animal is an animal that finds its own food. It looks after itself and does not need people to care for it. Can you say which of these animals are **not** wild ?

Angelfish

Flamingo

Salamander

Skunk

Giraffe

Spider

Badger

Kitten

Seahorse

Pig

Dog

Butterfly

Crocodile

Where animals live

Animals live almost everywhere –
in hot places and cold places, on
land, in the sea, on the tops of
high mountains, and even under
the ground. Polar bears live in the
freezing cold Arctic, in the far
north of the world. They have
thick furry coats to keep
them warm in the
ice and snow.

*Even baby polar
bears don't seem
to mind the cold!*

This lizard lives in the dry desert. It likes to bask on a rock in the burning hot sunshine. It feeds on insects and can make do with very little water to drink.

Polar bears hunt seals and birds.

How animals move

Most animals that live on land
have legs to walk, hop or run on.
The fastest land animal is the
cheetah.

Cheetah

Fish swim along by flicking their tails from side to side. They steer with their fins.

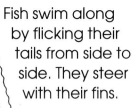

Gazelle

Birds fly by pushing against the air with their broad, flat wings.

Feeding

All animals need food to grow and stay alive. Animals that just eat plants are called herbivores. Other animals that feed mostly on meat are called carnivores.

Plant-eaters have to watch out for the meat-eaters!

Zebras eat grass . . .

. . . and lions eat zebras!

Many fierce-looking animals are herbivores, not carnivores. The gentle gorilla likes to munch on different kinds of leaves, shoots and fruit. Although gorillas are strong, they are also shy. They do not fight other animals if they can avoid it.

This brightly coloured parrot eats fruit and seeds.

Hunting

Many animals hunt in groups for food. These fierce killer whales are chasing a school of salmon. The whales herd the salmon into shallow water then dart among the trapped fish and eat as many as they can.

Killer whales hunt in groups called pods.

FISHY MOBILE

Make this mobile out of cardboard and shiny paper or foil.

1 Cut out a large fish and about 15 smaller ones from thin card.
2 Cover with shiny paper and make a hole in the top of each fish.
3 Use coloured thread or string to hang the fish from a coathanger.

Staying alive

For many animals, life is full of danger. They need ways to defend themselves, and their young, from hungry carnivores.

These musk oxen have sharp horns. If a pack of wolves tries to attack them, the oxen stand in a circle and lower their heads so that their horns point outwards like daggers.

The wasp uses a poisonous sting to defend itself. The porcupine (right) turns its back on its enemies and points its sharp quills at them.

Baby oxen are kept safe inside the circle.

Animal senses

Animal senses – sight, hearing, touch, smell and taste – are very important. Animals use them to find food and avoid enemies.

Snakes can smell their next meal through their tongues.

The panther's whiskers can sense the slightest touch.

S 320,968
591

Birds have very good eyesight. A buzzard high in the sky can spot a tiny beetle on the ground.

HUNTING IN THE DARK

Many night animals hunt by listening. Owls fly very quietly, and their ears can pick up the slightest sound.

How animals learn

As they grow up, animals need to learn how to find food and keep themselves safe. Most animals learn by watching and copying their parents.

A blue tit will spit out a poisonous caterpillar and remember that it tastes nasty.

Fox cubs find out how to chase and jump on prey by playing together.

The chimp catches the termites on the end of a stick.

This young chimp is discovering how to catch termites by watching its mother poke a stick deep into a termites' nest.

Animal groups

Many animals live in families or even bigger groups. They help each other to get food, to look after their young and to watch out for danger.

Baby elephants live with their mothers and other elephants in a herd.

Do you know the names of these animal groups?

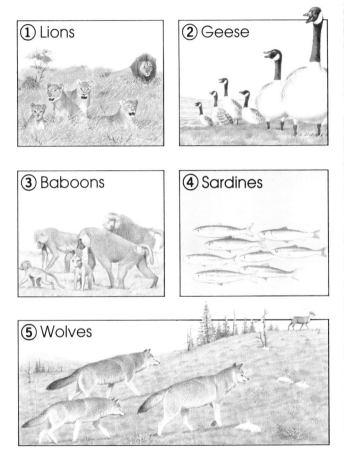

① Lions

② Geese

③ Baboons

④ Sardines

⑤ Wolves

ANSWERS 1 Pride **2** Flock
3 Troop **4** Shoal **5** Pack

25

Animals in danger

Many wild animals are in danger. We need to look after them, and the places in which they live, or they may become extinct.

There are few giant pandas alive today.

MODEL ANIMALS

Make a wriggly snake and lizard using this easy salt-dough mixture.

Salt-dough recipe: Mix together 340 grams plain flour, 100 grams salt, 350 ml water. Knead well to make a soft dough.

1 Roll out a long coil for the snake, thinner at one end. Model the lizard shape and add feet. Join the pieces of dough with a little water.

2 Press a pen top into the dough so it looks like scaly skin.

3 Bake at Gas Mark 3 (170°C) for about 2 hours.

4 When cool, paint in bright colours and varnish.

Some special words

Carnivore   An animal that just eats meat. It has sharp teeth for cutting and tearing food.

Extinct   Completely died out. If all of one kind of animal or plant disappears from the Earth, it becomes extinct.

Herbivore   A plant-eating animal. It has a mixture of sharp and flat teeth for cutting and grinding food.

Prey   The food of a carnivore or hunter. For example, a zebra is the prey of a lion or leopard.

Index